The Wegley Family History

By: Tracy Richardson

Johann Paul Wegerline came from Lampertheim, Bergstrasse, Hessen, Germany arriving in America on September 18, 1732, aboard the Johnson Galley of London. This is the story of their descendants starting with Philip Wagerline who was born in America in 1739 all the way to Raymond Edward Wegley who was born in 1925.

These are all the directly descendants of Philip Wagerline (1739-1831) and Anna Dorthea "Fronica" Krafft (1748-1792).

Copyright

No part of this book may be reproduced, reverse-engineered, transmitted in any form or by any means, graphic, electronic, or mechanical, including photocopy, recording, taping, or by any information storage or retrieval system, without the permission in writing from the publisher except in the case of brief quotation embodied in critical articles and reviews. Please respect the hard work of the author and do not post or share this work.

This book deals with the family history of the Wegley family. The data gathered to write this story was done through years of extensive genealogical research from countless sources including personal family histories. For clarification purposes, often certain sources will be cited throughout the book.

ISBN-13: 978-1717081476
ISBN-10: 1717081479

CONTENTS

INTRODUCTION

The Wegley family has a long and fascinating history. According to some sources it dates back to medieval times and can be traced to a prominent family that played a large part in shaping European history. But for our purposes, we are going to focus on the Wegley family that came to America.

Researching into the Wegley family isn't always an easy task. What complicates matters more than anything are the spelling variations of the family name. Historians call it "anglicizing" a name, which means when a family immigrates and has a complicated name, it often gets shortened either on purpose or because it was misspelled on accident.

In the most basic form, the German name of Wägeli becomes Wageli and eventually Wegley. But things are never that easy. There are at least 25 commonly found spellings of the Wegley name. There are others, obvious typos like Freigley and Sergley, but these 25 are more common and found numerous times through historical documents like birth certificates, marriage announcements, death notices, US census records, land grants, etc.

When you think of American history, you are all too quick to think of our British ancestors. We get our language, and much of our first government was formed from concepts taken from the British government. We were originally identified as the British colonies.

However, that being said, we shouldn't be so quick to forget that many great Americans came from all over and that includes Germany. So many of the of Colonial America success stories are thanks to the people of German origin, those that immigrated to America early in our history. This book will tell you the story of just one of those German families from the time they came to America until today.

It's amazing how far they have come and all they have accomplished along the way. They built bridges and settled towns. They were farmers and factory workers, mill workers and miners. They were the Wegley family, who to this day are still going strong.

So please let me introduce you to my family, starting with Philip, the first in my line born in America.

DISCLAIMER

Genealogical research is not an exact science. It's like a mystery, wrapped in an enigma wrapped in a pile of typographical errors and bad transcriptions.

I have worked tirelessly for years to gather the information resented to you here. Still, sometimes despite your best effort to try and connect Obtilia with Otilia and Otelia, things just fall apart. However, in an attempt to be as accurate as possible, if I don't have 100% proof of a fact, I either don't include it or explain that within the description of the listed family member.

This is also the reason I didn't start my book with Paul Wegerlin, Philip's father whose full name is most likely Johann Paul but changed to Paulus while immigrating to America and then later just simply Paul while in America because due to some conflicting information I just wasn't able to speak confidently about his entire life.

We have an obscure document (Germany, Select Births, and Baptisms, 1558-1898) that tell us Johann Paul Wegerlin and Ottilia had a child named Anna Clara Wegerlin. Then that same document shows they had another child, but this time they were listed as Johann Paul Wegerle and Ottilia instead of Wegerlin as with the birth of their daughter Anna Clara. When he came to America the (*Filby, P. William, ed. Passenger and Immigration Lists Index, 1500s-1900s. Farmington Hills, MI, USA: Gale Research, 2012 – page 34 source publication 1330.1*) gives us his name as Paulus Wegerlin – another transcription of the exact same document gives it to us at Paul Wegerline.

I've long been curious about the original name before we started making changes to it, and it seems like it most likely would have been Wägeli. However, there is a long history of variations on our names here is a short list that I found in just one batch of German records.

- Wegerlin
- Wegelin
- Wägerlin
- Wegerlein
- Wägele
- Wägeli
- Waegerlen
- Waegerlin
- Weckherlin
- Weekerlin
- Wegerle
- Weikhelin
- Wiegerlin
- Wigerli
- Wigerlin
- Waeckherlin
- Wuekherlin

PHILIP WAGERLINE

Philip Wagerline was born in 1739 in Lancaster County, Pennsylvania. He died on September 18, 1831 in Brothersvalley Township, Pennsylvania at the age of 92. He was my 5th great-grandfather.

By all accounts, Philip Wagerline was a colorful character. He not only was the first member of our family to be born in America, but he also was the oldest documented member of the town of Brothersvalley Township, Pennsylvania. This town is in Somerset County and is about 80 miles southeast of Pittsburgh.

Philip was born to Paul and Ottilia Wegerline. His father Paul (aka Palus) was originally from Lampertheim, Bergstrasse, Hessen, Germany and immigrated to America on September 18, 1732, when he was 33 years old. Palus arrived at the port of Philadelphia and stayed mostly in that area until his death 30 years later. He died in Lancaster County, Pennsylvania. This also happened to be where Philip was born in 1739.

His mother died in 1763 because the counter of Lancaster has some sort of document relating to her death and list her death as having taken place in 1763. They spell her name Obtilia Wegerlin.

We don't know the exact day Philip was born just the location and year which was in Lancaster County, Pennsylvania in 1739. Even though he lived nearly three hundred years ago, we still have a significant number of documents about his life in part because he was one of the founding members of the town.

Brothersvalley was organized as a township in 1771 in what was then Bedford County. Back then it included all the area which is the present-day county of Somerset. This was a huge territory that in modern day times would be broken up into several smaller townships. This is why often you see documents that refer to the same person living in Stoney Creek Glades, Berlin and Brothersvalley all at the same time.

Philip brought his family to the area that would become known as Brothersvalley before it was considered *safe for settlement.*

The brave people who came to Brothersvalley to make a home for their families during this period were true pioneers. They were moving into an unknown area where land had to be cleared so they could plant crops to eat and build cabins for shelter. Still, despite all the work they put into their new land, the future wasn't certain. At any time, the Native Americans could invade their land and hurt, or even worse, kill their entire family.

One of the earliest white settlers in the area was a man by the name of Mr. Dilbert. He had moved there from Carlisle, Pennsylvania with his family. He found a plot of land he liked and began to build it up. Things didn't go well for the Dilbert family though. In 1739 Dilbert's wife and children were slain by Native Americans, so he returned home to Carlisle.

There would be no white settlers again in the area until 1768 when Philip Wagerline brought his family and settled the area. They traveled about 170 miles from their original home in Lancaster County, Pennsylvania. This is where his children Catherine, Philip, Frederick, John, and Susanna were born, baptized and raised. Lancaster County was the only home they had ever known.

Originally, I wasn't sure what prompted Philip to travel so far with his entire family in tow to build a new home in the area, where he would help to found a town that still exists to this day, hundreds of years later.

However, I found an obscure book that later explained to me the reason for this move not only by Philip but others like him.

The book said there were two main reasons, first is they were German and wanted nothing to do with the impending war coming between the colonists and their lords of their homeland, England. They too were recently free from the bonds of government and taxation and the war in their homeland. They wanted the quiet and freedom of the wilderness.

Secondly, they were mainly Quakers, Mennonites, and Brethren, who did not believe in the taking up of arms so even if they did support the cause, they weren't looking to join in the battle.

Sometime between 1790 and 1800 Philip Wagerline changed his name to Philip Weigley. We aren't really sure why he made the change, but since there are so many accounts of Philip Wagerline's history, we are able to verify this is, in fact, the same person.

Philip Wagerline married Anna Dorothea Krafft on April 20, 1767. She went by the name "Fronica." Like her husband, she too came from German immigrants. In fact, she was born in Germany and came to America with her family.

Together they had at least six children.

- Susanna Eva (1769-1841)
- Frederick (1773-1836)
- Catharine (1774-1834)
- Philip (1775-1836)
- Joseph (1779-1836)
- John (1781-1836)

The move to Brothersvalley was a good one for Philip despite the fact that the area was known for its harsh weather. People say that there Brothersvalley has two seasons, August and winter. Brothersvalley lies in a high cup-shaped plateau, and as a result, the growing season is about four weeks shorter than nearby areas. The frost comes early and hangs late. They also had a lot of rain; it would come quickly and often, getting over 40 inches a year.

Still, despite the hardships, Philip did well. In 1773 just five years after moving to the area his family, the tax records show us that he owned 200 acres of land, 10 of which were cleared. This was not easy either because this was a time when he didn't have a lot of fancy technology to work the land, and it was all under constant threat of the nearby Native Americans.

During the 1790 US Census, we find Philip Wagerline living with his family in Bedford County, Pennsylvania. Their family at the time totaled eight members, 4 of which were males under 16, 2 were males 16 or over and 2 were females. That's all we really know from the 1790 United States Federal Census. Back then the census records weren't as detailed as they are today.

Year: 1790; Census Place: Bedford, Pennsylvania; Series: M637; Roll: 9; Page: 247; Image: 139; Family History Library Film: 0568149

Ten years later, we find the Philip is now listed as living in Brothersvalley, Pennsylvania. This is because the government started to identify the town by name now instead of just by county. This meant the town of Brothersvalley was growing and thus giving it more official recognition.

This particular census was called the Pennsylvania Septennial Census, and unlike the federal one, it only seems to list the adult males of the town.

Septennial Census Returns, 1779–1863. Box 1026, microfilm, 14 rolls. Records of the House of Representatives. Records of the General Assembly, Record Group 7. Pennsylvania Historical and Museum Commission, Harrisburg, PA.

Those who first came to the area known as Brothersvalley were German immigrants who were members of the Dunkard or German Baptist church, and referred to each other as "The Brethren," or "Brueders Lide."

Early on they had already begun calling the area they lived in "Brudersthal" – Brothersvalley and they called their church The Church of the Brethren.

The Brethren, an Anabaptist group, were an offshoot of Protestantism, which originally dissented from several Lutheran and Reformed churches.

The name Anabaptist means "one who baptizes again." Anabaptists are Christians who believe that baptism is valid only when the candidate confesses his or her faith in Christ and wants to be baptized. Their persecutors named them this, referring to the practice of baptizing persons when they converted or declared their faith in Christ, even if they had been baptized as infants.

They believed that that baptismal candidates be able to make a confession of faith that is freely chosen and so rejected baptism of infants, claiming that infant baptism was not part of scripture and was therefore null and void. They said that baptizing self-confessed believers was their first true baptism.

Philip died on September 18, 1831, at the ripe old age of 92. We know when he died and how old he was upon his death from his tombstone.

He was buried in the Weigley Cemetery which is located in Berlin, Pennsylvania. The Weigley Cemetery has a total of six graves, Philip (1821), Lucinda (1824), Elizabeth (1874), Seth (1889), and Susanna (1895).

About a year before Philip's death he wrote his will and here is what it says ...

WILL OF PHILIP WAGERLINE, DECEASED

IN THE NAME OF GOD AMEN. I PHILIP WAGERLINE THE ELDEST OF BROTHERS VALLEY TOWNSHIP, IN THE COUNTY OF SOMERSET, AND STATE OF PENNSYLVANIA YEOMAN BEING IN HEALTH OF BODY AND OF SOUND DISPOSING MIND MEMORY AND UNDERSTANDING BLESSED BE GOD FOR THE SAME. DO MAKE AND PUBLISH THIS MY LAST WILL AND TESTAMENT IN MANOR

AND FORM FOLLOWING TO WIT: FIRST IT IS MY WILL, AND I DO ORDER AND DIRECT THAT ALL MY JUST DEBTS, AND FUNERAL EXPENSES BE DULY PAID AND SATISFIED AS SOON AS CONVENIENTLY CAN BE AFTER MY DECEASE.

ITEMS I GIVE AND DEVISE UNTO MY SON PHILIP WAGERLINE HIS HEIRS AND ASSIGNS FOREVER.

ALL THAT CERTAIN PLANTATION AND TRACT OF LAND WHEREON HE NOW LIVES ACCORDING TO THE BOUNDARIES AS LAID OFF BY ACTUAL SURVEY INCLUDING THE PIECE OF MEADOW ORIGINALLY LAID OFF TO MY SON FREDERICK WAGERLINE

AS THE SAME IS FENCED OFF FOR WHICH SAID PIECE OF MEADOW THE SAID PHILIP WAGERLINE IS TO LAY OFF TO THE TRACT OF LAND SOLD BY THE SAID FREDERICK WAGERLINE UNTO MY SON JOHN WAGERLINE THE SAME QUANTITY OF LAND AT THE UPPER END OF THE PLACE NEXT TO THE TOWN OF BERLIN SO AS TO BE OF THE LEAST INJURY TO THE SAID PHILIP WAGERLINE'S PLANTATION THE SAID TRACT CONTAINING ABOUT TWO HUNDRED AND TWENTY ACRES BE THE SAME MORE OR LESS SITUATE IN BROTHERS VALLEY TOWNSHIP AFORESAID AND BOUNDED BY LANDS OF MICHAEL MOYER, JOHN WAGERLINE AND OTHERS TOGETHER WITH THE APPURTENANCES.

HE OR THE PAYING THERE OUT UNTO MY SON JOHN WAGERLINE AND HEIRS OR REPRESENTATIVES SIX HUNDRED DOLLARS THIRTY DAYS AFTER MY DECEASE: AND ALSO PAYING TO MY SON IN LAW PETER GLESSNER OR HIS HEIRS SEVEN HUNDRED DOLLARS, THREE HUNDRED DOLLARS ONE YEAR AFTER MY DECEASE AND TWO HUNDRED DOLLARS PER ANNUM UNTIL THE SAID SEVEN HUNDRED DOLLARS ARE PAID.

AND ALSO PAYING UNTO MY DAUGHTER SUSANA MARKLY TWO HUNDRED DOLLARS FOUR YEARS AFTER MY DECEASE.

ITEMS I GIVE AND DEVISE UNTO MY SON JOHN WAGERLINE ALL THAT CERTAIN PLANTATION AND TRACT OF LAND WHEREON HE NOW LIVES AS LAID OFF CONTAINING ABOUT ONE HUNDRED AND SIXTEEN ACRES TOGETHER WITH THE APPURTENANCES ADJOINING LANDS OF MICHAEL MOYER, PETER HAY, PHILIP WAGERLINE AND OTHERS TO HAVE AND TO HOLD THE SAME TO HIM HIS HEIRS AND ASSIGNS FOREVER AND ALSO MY EIGHT DAY CLOCK.

ITEMS I GIVE AND DEVISE UNTO MY SON FREDERICK WAGERLINE AND TO HIS HEIRS AND ASSIGNS THE PROCEEDS IN FULL WHICH AROSE FROM THE SALE OF A TRACT OF LAND THAT HE SOLD UNTO MY AFORESAID SON JOHN WAGERLINE AND WHICH PROCEEDS HE HATH HERETOFORE RECEIVED.

ITEMS I GIVE UNTO THE HEIRS OF MY SON-IN-LAW JOSEPH MARKLY, DECEASED, THE PROCEEDS IN FULL WHICH AROSE FROM THE SALE OF A TRACT OF LAND WARRANTED IN THE NAME OF SAMUEL DAVIDSON CONTAINING FOUR HUNDRED AND EIGHTY-NINE ACRES AND WHICH PROCEEDS THE SAID DECEASED HATH HERETOFORE RECEIVED.

AND ITEM IT IS MY WILL AND I DO ORDER AND DIRECT THAT MY SON JOHN WAGERLINE SHALL WITHIN THIRTY DAYS AFTER MY DECEASE DELIVER UP TO MY EXECUTOR HEREINAFTER NAMED ALL MY PERSONAL ESTATE THAT MAY BE WITHIN HIS POSSESSION OR KNOWLEDGE OF NATURE OR KIND SO EVER IT MAY BE OR THAT I AM IN ANYWISE ENTITLED TO AND IT IS MY WILL THAT THE SAID HEREIN AFTER NAMED EXECUTOR MAKE SALE AS SOON AS CONVENIENT OF SUCH PROPERTY AS MAY BE DELIVERED UNTO HIM BY MY SAID SON JOHN WAGERLINE AND THAT THE PROCEEDS THEREOF BE DIVIDED EQUALLY BETWEEN MY SON-IN-LAW PETER GLESSNER AND MY DAUGHTER SUSAN MARKLY AND LASTLY I NOMINATE CONSTITUTE AND APPOINT MY TRUSTY FRIEND JACOB GOOD OF BROTHERS VALLEY TOWNSHIP EXECUTOR OF THIS MY LAST WILL AND TESTAMENT HEREBY REVOKING ALL OTHER WILLS, LEGACIES AND BEQUESTS BY ME HERETOFORE MADE AND DECLARING THIS AND NO OTHER TO BE MY LAST WILL AND TESTAMENT.

Philip Wagerline and his wife had at least six children together. The crazy thing is that four of the six children died in 1836, two of which who died on the same day. This is something that caught my attention. I couldn't help but wonder what in the world could have possibly happened in 1836 to cause this to happen.

- Susanna Eva (1769-1841)
- Frederick (1773-1836)
- Catharine (1774-1834)
- Philip (1775-1836)
- Joseph (1779- 1836)
- John (1781-1836)

You will find Philip Wagerline in the 1790, 1800, 1810, 1820 and 1830 United States Federal Census. He was a farmer and despite slavery being common during this time, especially for farming families with a lot of acreage like he had, Philip never owned a single colored slave – at least not according to the census. He had hundreds of acres of land and worked it all on his own, or with his family.

We are able to confirm who his children are in large part to those census records and to his will. He first mentions Philip, then Fredrick, and then John. Then he talks about his son in low Peter Glessner who is husband to his daughter Catharine. Next, he makes mention of both his daughter Susanna and her husband, Joseph Markly. He does not make any mention of his son Joseph. However, we have birth records that very clearly tell us that Joseph is the son of Philip.

CHURCH BOOK OF CONGREGATIONS OF BOTH EVANGELICAL LUTHERAN AND EVANGELICAL REFORMED (BROTHERS VALLEY TOWNSHIP). TRANSCRIPT: REFERENCED ON PAGE 15 AS SON TO PHILIP WAGGELE, BORN 04 APR 1779. ISBN #0-933227-82-5

JOHAN FREDERIK WEIGLEY

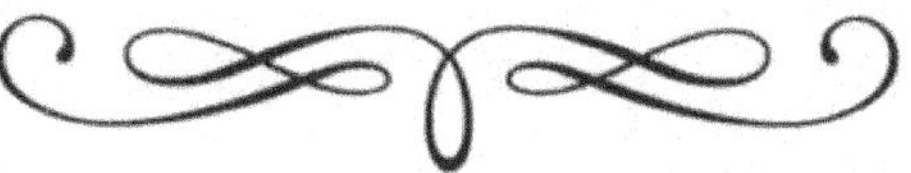

> Johan Frederick Weigley was born on May 22, 1773. He died in 1836 in Brothersvalley Township, Pennsylvania at the age of 63. He was my 4th great-grandfather.

Johan Frederik Weigley went by Frederik, but our first record of him comes from his christening, where it states that he was listed as Johan Fridrich Wegerlein.

It says he was christened at the Reformed Congregation, Hagerstown, Washington, Maryland. He was baptized on October 20, 1774. The record confirms his parents were Philip and *Fronica* and that the baptismal sponsor was Friedrich Kraft.

MARYLAND BIRTHS AND CHRISTENINGS, 1600–1995. INDEX. FAMILYSEARCH, SALT LAKE CITY, UTAH, 2009, 2010. INDEX ENTRIES DERIVED FROM DIGITAL COPIES OF ORIGINAL AND COMPILED RECORDS. FHL FILM NUMBER 14145.

The question is, why was Frederik christened in Hagerstown, Maryland when Philip was from Lancaster County and then later moved to Brothersvalley? Some have speculated that his father Philip could have gone to Brothersvalley to stake his claim in the property and then returned to fetch his family, traveling down into Maryland via Hagerstown along the way. Or quite simply they may have been visited by the Reformed Pastor from Hagerstown, Maryland as he sought to minister those living in rural areas.

There are so many variations in the spelling of Frederik's name. These variations in the spelling of his name, however, could be for a variety of reasons. First, it could have just been a bad transcription from a very old document, which might have been hard to read. It could have also been that the person who originally wrote down the name, wasn't sure himself (or herself) how to spell the name and just wrote it down how they thought it was spelled.

his was a long time ago and hundreds of years ago, not everyone could read and write. This is why we get so many crazy versions of names.

- Johan Friedrich
- Johan Fridrich Wegerlein
- Johan Frederik Weigley
- Frederic Weigley

We first find Frederik in the 1800 census when he was living with his wife, Catharine. There he is listed as Frederic Weigley.

In 1810 he's listed as Frederick Wegley. By then all of his children were born, and there were a total of seven people living in his household, which one would assume that would include him and his wife and his five children.

- Anna Maria (Feb 26, 1801)
- Joseph William (October 14, 1802)
- Henrietta (November 2, 1804)
- Lydia (January 10, 1807)
- Theresa (September 16, 1809)

The problem with old census records is that it didn't give anyone other than the name of the head of household. So, while we may know he had a female living with him under 16, we wouldn't know for sure what her name was, at least not with just the census records.

Johan Frederik Weigley went by Frederik died in 1836 when he was 63 years old. Although we don't know what killed him, we do know that like 3 of his other siblings who also died that same year, he was sick.

I was never able to find a will listed in his name in the available records for that time.

THE GREAT YET UNSOLVED 1836 MYSTERY

While doing my research on Philip Wagerline, I noticed that four of his six children died in the year 1836, two of which appeared to have died on the exact same day. That struck me as odd.

- Susanna Eva (1769-1841)
- Frederick (1773-1836)
- Catharine (1774-1834)
- Philip (17751836)
- Joseph (1779-1836)
- John (1781-1836)

I wanted to know how why they died but finding out turned out not to be as easy as one might think. I couldn't find any reference to cause of death in the documents I had available to me at the time. I did find the will of one of Philip's kids who died in 1836 who referenced being sick although he didn't say exactly what his illness was.

So, I wondered what about other people. I mean there couldn't be that many people living in Brothersvalley Township, PA in the year 1836, right?

The first thing I did was look up the historic population. When the town was founded in 1773, they did the first official tax assessment, and they listed a total of 41 households – although I should mention that 18 of the 41 were inmates – meaning at the time there were only 23 freemen.

Last Name	First Name	Status
ABRAHAMS	Gabriel	Freemen
BLACK	James	Freemen
BOWMAN	John	Freemen
BRUNER	George	Freemen
BRUNER	Henry	Freemen
HASKIN	William	Freemen
HAY	Frances	Freemen
HENDERSON	Edward	Freemen
HENDRIX	John	Freemen
HIGGINS	Edward	Freemen
HINEBAUGH	John	Freemen
HOGLAND	James	Freemen
JENNINGS	Joseph	Freemen
JUDY	Matthew	Freemen
OGLE	Thomas	Freemen
PURSLEY	Danie	Freemen
SHINDLER	George	Freemen

			en
SHINDLER	Henry	en	Freem
ST. CLAIR	John	en	Freem
STOY	Caspar	en	Freem
WELLS	Richard	en	Freem
WINGART	Jacob	en	Freem
WORRELL	Atwel	en	Freem

First Assessment, Brothersvalley Twp., 1773. Head of Household Only. This county is part of the USGenWeb Project, a non-profit genealogical resource web system, and is maintained by April Phillips and Connie Burkett with help and information provided by other volunteers.

By 1779 Brothersvalley had grown from 24 households to 176, and the government was collecting taxes on over 23,000 acres of land. Still, 176 households aren't that many, so several people all dying the same year should stick out, or so I would assume.

I was unable to find any tax records for Brothersvalley Township for 1830-1840 for this area, however, I did find the 1850 federal census for Brothersvalley Township.

Since there are also no death certificates for them during this time period, I began to look for references to a will from any of the four children who died in 1836, which was Johan Frederick, Philip Jr., Joseph or John.

I was able to locate Philip's will. Philip Jr. and his brother Joseph both seem to have died on the same day,

October 26, 1836. Here is the transcription of his will. Please note some of the misspellings are just because that is how they appeared in his will.

IN THE NAME OF GOD AMEN. I PHILIP WEAGLEY OF BROTHERS VALLEY TOWNSHIP SOMERSET COUNTY OF STATE OF PENNSYLVANIA (PRAISED BE GOD FOR THE SAME) AND BEING DECIDED TO SETTLE MY WORLDLY AFFAIRS WHILE I HAVE STRENGTH AND CAPACITY SO TO DO.

DO MAKE AND PUBLISH THIS MY LAST WILL AND TESTAMENT. AND JUST AND PRINCIPALLY I COMMIT MY LOVE UNTO THY HANDS OF MY CREATOR WHO GAVE IT AND MY BODY TO THE EARTH. AND AS TO SUCH WORLDLY ESTATE WHEREWITH IT HATH PLEASED GOD TO ENTRUST ME I DISPOSE OF ALL OF THE SAME AS FOLLOWS TO MY FIRST ITEM I WILL THAT ALL OF MY JUST DEBTS AND FUNERAL EXPENSES SHALL BE PAID BY MY EXECUTOR OR HEREINAFTER MENTIONED.

THE SECOND ITEM I GIVE UNTO MY BELOVED WIFE ELISABETH THE ONE HALF OF ALL MY ESTATE REAL AND PERSONAL.

THIRDLY I GIVE UNTO MY FRIEND GEORGE KNEPPER INTERMARRIED TO TRACY WEAGLEY FIVE HUNDRED DOLLARS.

FOURTHLY I GIVE AND BEQUEATH UNTO ELISA WEIGLEY THE DAUGHTER OF POLLY CROFT WHO HAS SINCE BEEN MARRIED TO HER HUSBAND NAME NOT KNOWN THE SUM OF FIVE HUNDRED DOLLARS.

FIFTHLY I GIVE AND BEQUEATH UNTO MY BROTHER FREDERICK FOUR HUNDRED DOLLARS.

SIXTHLY I GIVE AND BEQUEATH UNTO MY SISTER CATHARINE GLESSNER'S CHILDREN EACH ONE HUNDRED DOLLARS.

SEVENTHLY I GIVE AND BEQUEATH UNTO MY BROTHER JOHN WEAGLEY CASH ONE HUNDRED DOLLARS.

FURTHER, MY EXECUTORS SHALL AFTER MY DEATH PROCEED TO SELL ALL MY PERSONAL PROPERTY OTHER THAN SUCH AS MY WIFE MAY THINK TO TAKE AT THE APPRAISEMENT WHICH SHALL BE CONSIDERED A PART OF HER SHARE AS SOON AFTER MY DEATH AS THE SHALL THING PROPER.

Further as to my real estate my will is that the plantation whereion I now live shall not be sold under 5 years after my death which my will is shall be farmed by Seth (Leth??) Weigley as such to give my wife one third of all the grain hay apples and all that is raised on the plantation with such such pasture and privledged in the barn and stable as she may want with such privlege with the house and garden milk (mill??) house and the yard and as she may want furtheR the said Leeth (Seth????) Weigley shall keep the fences in repair and make such new fences as shall be necessary.

Further my executors shall commence paying as follows as soon as conveniently can be done first with Elisa Weigley, Daughter of Polly Craft, Second then to George Knepper married to Tracy Weigley then thirdly to my brother Fredrick all to be paid with the sums aforementioned then the balance bequeAthed unto my sister Cahteraine's children and my brother John's children if it can NOt be paid out of my personal property as before mentioned then in such case they shall wait for their sum until the real estate is sold.

Further, all the balance remaining after paying over the above legacy's I give and bequeath unto my bother John's children.

Further should the said Leth (Seth?) Weigley not agree to farm the said planTation then in such case my executors shall rent it with the full intents and meaning as before mentioning further I do hereby appoint my Firstly friends Tobias Mujer (Mustler/MILLER???) and George Walker Esquire my executors of this my last will and testament and revoking all other wills declaring this last will and testament.

In witness where of I the testator have to this my will set my hand and seal this 19th day of October AD 1836. Signed sealed and in the presence of the testator and at his request John Brubaker (??) and MILFORD RiFur (??????).

His will as filed in Somerset County on the first day of November 1836. It was a handwritten will and here is what is actual signature looked like.

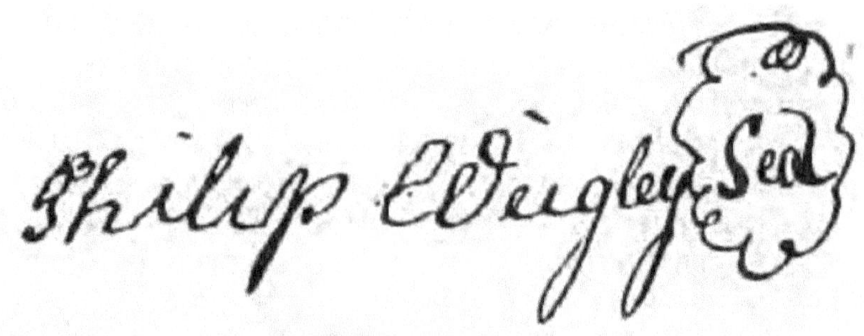

The Tobias mentioned as the executor of his will could be Tobias Miller who married his aunt Otilia or then again, they could have had a son and named him Tobias as well. Then again there is a "Mustler" on the tax rolls for Brothersvalley Township during that period so it could be that. I honestly just couldn't transcribe it.

He gave away a lot of money in his will. After giving half of everything, he owns to his wife he gave had the cash to cover his funeral expenses, plus an additional $2,500 in cash. That today would be worth about $67,000. That's a huge amount of cash for someone to have in 1836. Looks like he did very well for himself considering he was a farmer.

He gave more than a year's wages to those in his will. At this time in history, most people earned less than $400 a year.

He signed his will on October 19, 1836. He died a few days later, on October 26th. He was 61 years old.

This meant he knew he was dying. He knew he was sick, bad sadly I still can't figure out what he could have been sick with, which maybe could explain why the four siblings died so close together. In the end, I could never figure out how four of Philip's six children all died in the same year. It's a mystery that at least for now must be left unsolved.

JOSEPH WILLIAM WEGLEY

Joseph William Wegley was born on October 14, 1802. He died in June of 1879 in McKean, Pennsylvania. He was my 3rd great-grandfather.

Joseph William Wegley is the first member of my family to spell his name as "Wegley". He married Eva Berkebile in 1832.

Eve and Joseph Wegley ? Ca. 1850

We can also confirm this as a fact because their daughter Mary Amanda listed as such on her death certificate.

Joseph is listed in the and 1840 and 1850 United States Federal Census. In 1840 he was 48 years old and his wife Eve was 39. The 1850 United States Federal Census also gave us the name of each of his children and their ages.

- Theresa (19)
- Jonathan (14)
- Josiah (11)
- Susanna (10)
- Frederick (6)
- Adeline (5)
- Amanda (2)

During this time Eve's mother Elizabeth (who was 61 at the time) was also living with them.

It is with the 1860 United States Federal Census that we learn that Joseph and Eve had two more children, Austin and John Wesley, making Joseph William and Eva the proud parents of nine beloved Wegley children.

By the time Joseph William was 68, during the 1870 United States Federal Census, we learn that he was still living with his wife Eva and with his son John, which would have been his youngest child. All other residents have moved out by that time, presumably to marry and have families of their own.

We also learn that Joseph William can't read or write, and his occupation was listed as a Wood Chopper.

The U.S. Federal Census Mortality Schedules, 1850-1885 tell us that Joseph William Wegley died at the age of 79. His cause of death was listed as "old age" and that he died in McKean County, Pennsylvania.

JOHN WESLEY WEGLEY

John Wesley Wegley was the youngest child of Joseph William and Eva Berkebile. He's the first member of my family where I was able to get my hands on his actual death certificate. We also have the death certificates of two of his children, giving us further documentation of his family members.

John Wesley Wegley married Helen Elizabeth "Bessie" Swanson on June 18, 1885, in Warren County, Pennsylvania. She seems to be an immigrant from Sweden, who came to the country in 1880 (or 1881) which was just a few years prior to their marriage.

Which I should note that German was the most important foreign language spoken in Sweden prior to the Second World War after which English replaced German as the dominant foreign language spoken in the country.

Together John Wesley Wegley and Bessie had eight children, 6 of which were still alive by 1910. The two children we don't know of seemed to have died before 1900.

- Minerva "Minnie" Pearl (23)
- Frederick (21)
- Ruth Leona (16)
- John Clarence (10)
- Raymond (8)
- Howard (6)

John Wesley was working for some time as a Grocer. He would later change jobs and work in the oil and gas industry. In fact, when he died his occupation was listed as "Oil & Gas Producer."

John Wesley and his family lived at 507 Biddle Street, Kane Pennsylvania, a house that still stands to this day. The house was built in 1890 and today is 2,258 square feet and sits on an 8,276 square foot lot. I'm unsure if that was the original size or if modifications were made to it later in history. As of now, the home is a 6-bedroom 2-story home with two kitchens (former two apartment), two full baths, full basement, detached 2 & 3-car garages.

John Wesley died on December 15, 1972, from a cerebral hemorrhage, due to high blood pressure. In other words, he died from a stroke.

CERTIFICATE OF DEATH

COMMONWEALTH OF PENNSYLVANIA
DEPARTMENT OF HEALTH
BUREAU OF VITAL STATISTICS

File No. 116965

1. PLACE OF DEATH

County of McKean
Township of Hamlin
or
Borough of
or
City of

Registration District No. 682
Primary Registration District No. 3003
Registered No. 16

[If death occurred in a hospital or institution give its NAME instead of street and number.]

2. FULL NAME John W. Wrigley
(a) Residence No. 507 Bidette Kane Pa. St. Pa. Ward.
(Usual place of abode) (If nonresident give city or town and State)
Length of residence in city or town where death occurred 60 yrs. mos. ds. How long in U. S. if of foreign birth? yrs. mos. ds.

PERSONAL AND STATISTICAL PARTICULARS

3. SEX Male
4. COLOR OR RACE White
5. SINGLE, MARRIED, WIDOWED OR DIVORCED (write the word) Widowed

5a. If married, widowed, or divorced HUSBAND of (or) WIFE of Mrs. J. W. Wrigley

6. DATE OF BIRTH (month, day, and year) June 29 1858

7. AGE Years 69 Months 5 Days 16 IF LESS than 1 day ... hrs. or ... min.

8. OCCUPATION OF DECEASED
(a) Trade, profession or particular kind of work Oil & Gas Producer
(b) General nature of industry, business, or establishment in which employed (or employer)
(c) Name of employer

9. BIRTHPLACE (city or town) United States
(State or country)

10. NAME OF FATHER Joseph Wrigley

11. BIRTHPLACE OF FATHER (city or town) U. S.
(State or country) United States

12. MAIDEN NAME OF MOTHER Eva Birkibile

13. BIRTHPLACE OF MOTHER (city or town)
(State or country) United States

14. Informant Fred Wrigley
(Address) Kane Penna

15. Filed 2-18-27 Hartley H. Adair Registrar

MEDICAL CERTIFICATE OF DEATH

16. DATE OF DEATH December 15th 1927
(Month) (Day) (Year)

17. I HEREBY CERTIFY, That an inquest was held upon the body of the above named deceased on the 15th day of December 1927; That the jury rendered a verdict giving the cause of death as follows:

Cerebral hemmorhage apoplexy died very sudden without the attendance of a doctor

Sudden (duration) yrs. mos. ds.

CONTRIBUTORY (Secondary) High blood pressure
Long (duration) 2 yrs. mos. ds.

18. Where was disease contracted if not at place of death?
Did an operation precede death? No Date of
Was there an autopsy? No
What test confirmed diagnosis? Witness statement
(Signed) H. C. Heffner Coroner
Dec 15 1927 (Address) Bradford Pa.

*State the Disease Causing Death, or in deaths from Violent Causes, state (1) Means and Nature of Injury, and (2) whether Accidental, Suicidal, or Homicidal. (See reverse side for additional space.)

19. PLACE OF BURIAL, CREMATION OR REMOVAL Forest Lawn Cemetery
DATE OF BURIAL Dec 19-27

20. UNDERTAKER H. O. Lantz
ADDRESS Mt. Jewett Pa.

(OVER)

FREDRICK WEGLEY

> Fredrick Wegley was born on August 20, 1889 in Kane, Pennsylvania. He died on November 28, 1950 when he was 60 years old. He was my great-grandfather.

Fredrick Wegley was born on August 20, 1890, in Kane, Pennsylvania. He also has been known to spell his name as Fredrich Wegley. When he signed his World War II draft registration card, he spelled it at Fredrich Wegley, however on his gravestone you'll find it listed as Frederick Wegley.

REGISTRATION CARD—(Men born on or after April 28, 1877 and on or before February 16, 1897)

The 1910 United States Federal Census lists Frederick as 21, meaning he would have been born in about 1889 or 1890. However, his World War 1 Draft Registration Card states that he was born on August 20, 1887. But then again, he could have just lied so that he could go fight in the war. That was common back then.

I found his US Social Security Application claim, and that stated his date of birth as August 20, 1890. Then again, his World War II draft registration card lists his date of birth as August 20, 1889. Why I settled on August 20, 1889, was because that is what appears on his tombstone.

He married Tillie Blanch Edwards on February 4, 1920. There are several documents that confirm their marriage including their daughter Ruth's own marriage when she was 21. The document confirms both her mother and father's names and that they lived (at the time) in Belle Vernon, PA.

Their marriage seems to have taken place in Huntington, Cabell, West Virginia for some reason, even though they were both born in Pennsylvania.

"WEST VIRGINIA MARRIAGES, 1853–1970." INDEX. FAMILYSEARCH, SALT LAKE CITY, UTAH, 2008, 2009. DIGITAL IMAGES OF ORIGINALS HOUSED IN COUNTY COURTHOUSES IN VARIOUS COUNTIES THROUGHOUT WEST VIRGINIA. MARRIAGE RECORDS.

Together Fredrick and Tillie had six children.

- John Wesley (1923)
- Betty (1924)
- Raymond Edward (1925)
- Ruth Minerva (1928)
- Dora Mae (1930)
- Gretta (1935)

In 1940 they were living in Clarksburg, West Virginia where they moved to in about 1935 from Westmoreland, Pennsylvania. Fredrick worked as a Glass Cutter, and they rented their home. This is something he did back in Pennsylvania as well. During the 1930 United States Federal Census, he stated he worked as a Cutter in a Glass Factory.

He could read and write however he didn't graduate high school. He seems to have only completed his 3rd year of high school.

World War I lasted from July 28, 1914, to November 11, 1918, however, the U.S. didn't enter the war until April 6, 1917, after the sinking of seven U.S. merchant ships by German submarines and the revelation that the Germans were trying to get Mexico to make war with us.

On June 5, 1917, Fredrick Wegley went to register for the draft. It was with that document we learned the was a member of the national guard in the infantry division for the previous year.

Fredrick Wegley lived during the great depression which began in 1929. We see that by the US Federal Census he was working as a cutter in a glass factory in both 1930 and 1940. In 1940 his family of 8 was living off of about $4 a day. This obviously wasn't enough to survive so the whole family had to pitch in and this meant even the youngest went out and did any job they could to make money. My grandfather Raymond Edward who would be 15 in 1940 talked about working 2 or 3 jobs just to have food to eat.

When World War II broke out, Fredrick went to register for the draft again, despite his advance years.

It is this report that tells us that Fredrick Wegley was not a tall man. In fact, he was only 5 feet 7 ½ inches tall. He weighed 138 pounds. He had brown hair, grey eyes, and a ruddy complexion.

RUDDY IS USED TO DESCRIBE SOMETHING THAT IS REDDISH — LIKE THE COLOR OF RED HAIR, TOMATOES, OR YOUR CHEEKS ON A COLD WINTER'S DAY. RUDDY IS COMMONLY USED TO DESCRIBE SOMEONE'S COMPLEXION. IN THIS CASE, IT DESCRIBES A HEALTHY, REDDISH GLOW. YOUR SKIN MIGHT HAVE A RUDDY TONE FROM WORKING OUTSIDE.

I only mention his height because like my grandfather, Fredrick was a few inches shorter than the average male who is about 5 feet 9 and a half inches tall.

Fredrick died in 1950 and was buried in a grave in Okmulgee, Oklahoma where his youngest son, Raymond was living at the time. His wife Tillie would go on to live a long life and die in 1984. She was buried nearby.

RAYMOND EDWARD WEGLEY

My grandfather, Raymond Edward Wegley was born just before the start of the great depression, which officially began in 1929. He could both read and write and attended Belle Vernon High School.

Raymond appears in the 1930 United States Federal Census. At the time he was only a child at around four years old and living with his family in Westmoreland County, Pennsylvania.

In the 1940 United States Census he's now 14 and in the 7th grade. At this time his father was bringing in about $4 a day working in a glass factory, or around $1,500 a year. This is why, even at his young age he was out there hustling, working 2 and sometimes three jobs just to help bring food home so his family could survive. You just can't raise six kids on about $4 a day, even back then.

Raymond joined the war on November 29, 1943, at the age of 17 and was officially discharged on April 28, 1946. His brother John W. Wegley entered service the month before on February 19, 1943, but he went into the army.

The Wegley's seemed to be on the short side of things, which perhaps is why my mother and I ended up being only 5 feet tall ourselves. It's thanks to his draft registration that we know he was 5 feet 6 inches tall, with brown hair and blue eyes, just like his father and older brother, John Wesley.

Raymond was a Sergeant First Class and was awarded several medals for his service to his country. He served on the USS Earl K. Olsen (DE-765).

He served his country for three long years; he was officially and honorably discharged on April 28, 1946.

Just a few years later, Raymond married Elsie Jane Hoag on June 5, 1948, in Pennsylvania.

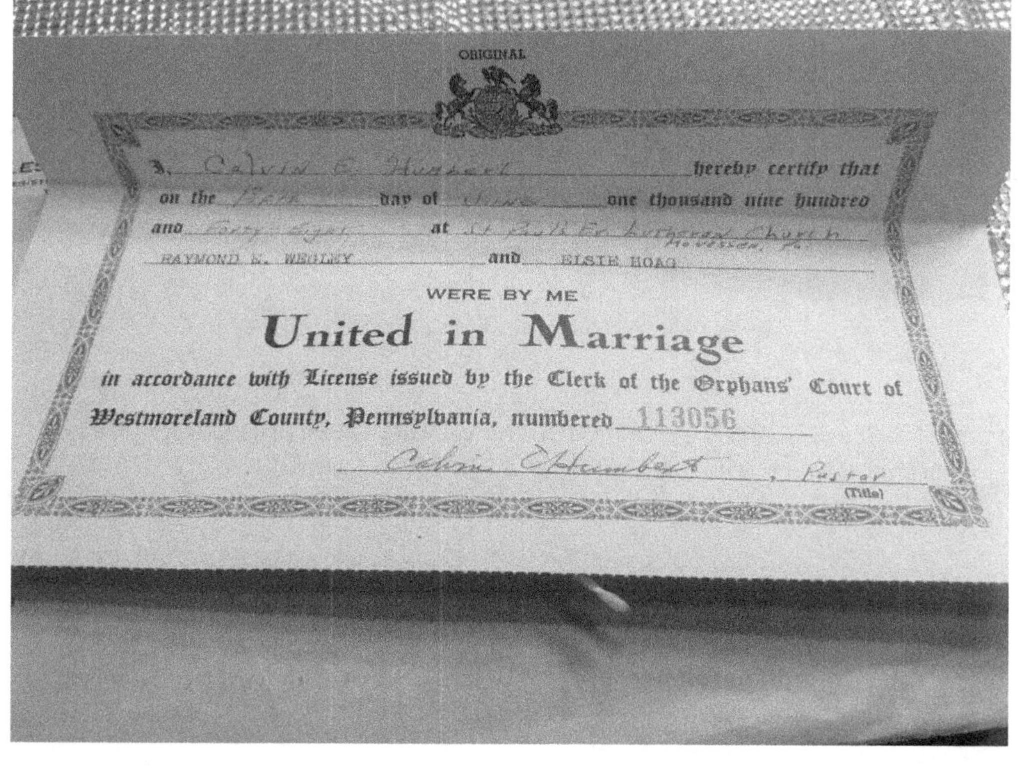

ORIGINAL
I, Calvin E. Humbert hereby certify that
on the 5th day of June one thousand nine hundred
and Forty-Eight at St. Paul's Ev. Lutheran Church
McKeesport, Pa.
RAYMOND E. WEGLEY and ELSIE HOAG
WERE BY ME
United in Marriage
in accordance with License issued by the Clerk of the Orphans' Court of
Westmoreland County, Pennsylvania, numbered 113056
Calvin Humbert , Pastor
(Title)

Together they had four children.

- Thomas Eugene (June 13, 1949)
- Karen Marie (January 26, 1951)
- Raymond Edward (Jr.) (December 11, 1952)
- Robert Thomas (September 27, 1954)

He worked for many years at the Bartlett Collins glass factory in Sapulpa, Oklahoma. He officially retired in April of 1989.

TAKEN ON THE VERY LAST DAY OF WORK IN 1989. THE LAST TIME HE CLOCKED OUT.

Just three years later he would die in his sleep of a heart attack on December 4, 1992.

JOHN WESLEY WEGLEY

> John Wesley Wegley was born on March 5, 1923 in Charleston, West Virginia. He died on November 1, 1982 in Henryetta, Oklahoma. He was my great-uncle – the brother of my maternal grandfather.

John Wesley Wegley was born on March 5, 1923, in Charleston, West Virginia. He is the 2nd John Wesley Wegley in my family tree, as he shares the same name as his grandfather. His father was Fredrick Wegley and his mother, Tillie Blanch Edwards.

Although John Wesley was born in West Virginia, he wasn't there long. By 1930 we find him with his family already living in Westmoreland County, Pennsylvania, thanks to the 1930 United States Federal Census.

He was seven years old at the time and as you might expect, attending school. He, however, wouldn't graduate high school. Times were hard in this period in history, and he had to quick high school after his 2nd year.

At 17 years old he was working in a glass factory just like his father. This was a new job for him because we can see in 1939, he had listed 0 hours work, and that is usual occupation is "new worker."

On February 12, 1943, John Wesley Wegley enlisted in the US Army. His enlistment term was for the duration of the

War or other emergency, plus six months, subject to the discretion of the President or otherwise according to law.

It is on his draft registration card that we learn he was 5 feet 5 inches tall with light complexion, brown hair, and blue eyes.

At the age of 23, John Wesley Wegley married Norman Jean Pocky. She was 21 years of age at the time. Their marriage took place on April 1, 1946, in Virginia.

CERTIFICATE OF MARRIAGE
COMMONWEALTH OF VIRGINIA

CITY / COUNTY OF Winchester

CLERK'S NO. 279

FULL NAME OF GROOM: J. Wesley Wegley

PRESENT NAME OF BRIDE: Norma Jean Pocky

MAIDEN NAME: Norma Jean Pocky

	GROOM				BRIDE		
AGE	RACE	SINGLE, WIDOWED, OR DIVORCED	NO. TIMES PREV. MARRIED	AGE	RACE	SINGLE, WIDOWED, OR DIVORCED	NO. TIMES PREV. MARRIED
23	W	Single	---	21	W	Single	---

OCCUPATION: Cutter — INDUSTRY OR BUSINESS: Window glass

OCCUPATION: Bookkeeper — INDUSTRY OR BUSINESS:

BIRTHPLACE: Charleston, W. Va.

BIRTHPLACE: Speers, Pa.

FATHER'S FULL NAME: Fred Wegley

FATHER'S FULL NAME: William Pocky

MOTHER'S MAIDEN NAME: Tillie Edwards

MOTHER'S MAIDEN NAME: Alice Frocheur

RESIDENCE: CITY OR COUNTY MAILING ADDRESS: 210 Wood St. Belle Vernon, Pa.

RESIDENCE: CITY OR COUNTY MAILING ADDRESS: 1003 Lower Crest Charleroi, Pa.

Date of Proposed Marriage: April 1, 1946

Place of Proposed Marriage: Winchester, Va.

Given under my hand this 1st day of April, 19 46.

Clerk of Corporation Court.

CERTIFICATE OF DATE AND PLACE OF MARRIAGE

I, E. T. Clark, a Minister of the Baptist (Denomination) Church, or religious order of that name, do certify that on the 1st day of Apr, 1946 City or Co. Winchester, Virginia, under authority of this license, I joined together in the Holy State of Matrimony the persons named and described therein. I qualified and gave bond according to law authorizing me to celebrate the rites of marriage in the county (or city) of Winchester, Commonwealth of Virginia.

Given under my hand this 1st day of April, 1946

Address of celebrant Winchester, Va.

E. T. Clark
(Person who performs ceremony sign here.)

It is in this document we get further proof that his parents were Fred and Tillie Wegley.

Together John Wesley and his beloved wife Norma Jean had two children, Lynn (born in 1947) and Wesley (born in 1952).

He died on November 1, 1982, when he was just 59 years old. He was buried in Henryetta, Oklahoma.

Name Reference

Paul Wegerline (1699)

Obtilia Wegerline (1701)

- Philip Wagerline (1739)
- Ana Dorthea Krafft (1748)

Susanna Eva (1769)

Johan Frederik (1731)

Catharine (1774)

Philip (1775)

Joseph (1779)

John (1781)

- Johan Frederik Weigley (1731)
- Catharine (1775)

Anna Marie (1801)

Joseph William (1802)

Henrietta (1804)

Lydia (1807)

Theresa (1809)

- Joseph William (1802)
- Eve Berkebile (1811)

Theresa (1831)

Jonathan (1834)

Josiah (1837)

SUSANNA (1841)

FREDERICK (1843)

ADELINE (1845)

MARY AMANDA (1847)

AUSTIN (1851)

JOHN WESLEY (1858)

- JOHN WESLEY WEGLEY (1858)
- HELEN ELIZABETH SWANSON (1865)

MINERVA PEARL (1887)

FREDRICK (1890)

RUTH LEONA (1893)

CLARENCE JOHN LEROY (1898)

RAYMOND (1900)

HOWARD (1903)

- FREDRICK WEGLEY (1890)
- TILLIE BLANCH EDWARDS (1899)

JOHN WESLEY (1932)

BETTY (1924)

RAYMOND EDWARD (1925)

RUTH MINERVA (1928)

DORA MAE (1930)

GRETTA (1935)